Breaking the Code of Silence

Breaking the Code of Silence

*A Journey from the Nefarious Crime Zone
Towards the Beloved Community*

Rhoda Johnson

Copyright © 2023 by Rhoda Johnson.

Library of Congress Control Number:	2023903328
ISBN: Hardcover	978-1-6698-6524-7
Softcover	978-1-6698-6863-7
eBook	978-1-6698-6525-4

All rights reserved. No part of this book may be reproduced or transmitted in any form or by any means, electronic or mechanical, including photocopying, recording, or by any information storage and retrieval system, without permission in writing from the copyright owner.

Any people depicted in stock imagery provided by Getty Images are models, and such images are being used for illustrative purposes only.
Certain stock imagery © Getty Images.

Print information available on the last page.

Rev. date: 02/28/2023

To order additional copies of this book, contact:
Xlibris
844-714-8691
www.Xlibris.com
Orders@Xlibris.com
830849

To Peacolia Dancy Barge, Ruffer Johnson, and Norma Downs Carson

CONTENTS

Acknowledgements..ix
Prologue..xi
Introduction..xv

Chapter 1 Spiritual Underpinnings...1
Chapter 2 Understanding the Nefarious Zone 7
Chapter 3 Know Yourself and Others 14
Chapter 4 Challenges, Surprises, and Lessons Learned 20
Chapter 5 Building Character...27
Chapter 6 Behavioral Change 33
Chapter 7 Navigating the Juvenile Criminal Zone 39
Chapter 8 Human Trafficking and the Nefarious Zone 44

Afterword: An Invitation to Dialogue 53
Bibliography...59

Acknowledgements

To produce any creative endeavor, it takes a village. My mother was the main member of my village. She nagged and cajoled me into finishing many a project. Yet my motivator has passed away, and I was left to my own devices. Often, I used my mother's words to keep me on target, but soon realized that I belonged to a large village that supported my efforts to formulate the thesis of this book. I would like to extend a special word of thanks and appreciation to those communities and the special people in them.

First, my family village which includes the Barge, Johnson, and Dancy families. To Peacolia Dancy and Foy Barge Sr; to Ruffer; to Ryan and Robert; to Foy Jr and Robert Mansfield; to Caroline; and to Deborah and Clarice, I extend my most heartfelt appreciation because you provided me with an intellectual, creative, and artistic cocoon in which to thrive.

I want to give a special thank you to my granddaughter Jiana Mari Lovenia. She inspired this book and provided me access to the special world that expanded my thinking. I was also motivated to make a better world for my other granddaughter Autiena and my great grandson Jorge. They were crucial to my efforts to complete this work.

The motivation to complete this book came in the form of my writing group, called Dirt Roads, and my membership/leadership in several organizations, such as Cornerstone Christian Fellowship, the West Mid Alabama Community Development Corporation (WMA-CDC), the 21st Century Leadership Movement, Department of Women's Studies, and the Coalition of Alabamians Rebuilding Education (C.A.R.E.). Without these organizations, I do not believe that I would have been able to successfully formulate the ideas in this book.

A special thanks goes out to my friend Dorothy Askew for being a sounding board for my ideas and providing me moral and spiritual support. I did not have the courage to let anyone read the manuscript, but Dorothy was the one person who knew most of what was in it. My friends also included the colleagues that I worked with as well. They include in no order: Martha Hawkins, Sophia Bracy Harris, Norma Downs Carson, Gladys Lyles-Gray, Hank Sanders, Faya Rose Toure, Carol Prejean and John Zippert, John H. England, Jr, Patricia Smith, William D. Matthews, Marilyn Culliver Armstead, Tommie Armstead, Joel Sogol, Phadra Carson Foster, Calvin Ross Culliver, and Jamelia Culliver Kelly.

I would also like to thank the two people, Deborah H. Walker, and Martha Morgan, who shared their wisdom with me in the interviews that I conducted in preparation for the book. Their insight into the struggle to implement change in our communities helped to guide my work and formulate a deeper analysis of the problems confronting us.

Last, but not least, I extend a great big thank you to my very capable and efficient Xlibris team, Sid Wilson, Emman Villaran, Bonnie Culver, Dawn Gibson, Tony McMillan, and Louise Panelo. Although an academic, my experience with the book world was mainly involved with the publication of journal articles. I was very new and inexperienced. They helped me through the process and held my hand along the way. Thank you so much for your encouragement.

I am sure that I have left out someone who contributed greatly to this work, but please know that it was not intentional. You could have said a word of encouragement or provided me with an important idea. Just know that you were valuable to my thought process and the completion of this book. I know my limitations and thank you from the bottom of my heart for helping me on this journey.

Prologue

The Nefarious crime Zone is that place where evil and depravity reign. It is that place where vile conduct and characteristics are normal; where time-honored laws and traditions are flagrantly violated. It is the place that most people think of as a myth and legend. It is euphemistically called the *twilight zone* or the *Bermuda Triangle*. There are many paths to get there, and it is easiest for those who are already in a precarious state.

If you are poor or a minority, your path is very slippery. You are already outside of the *magic circle*. Many in the dominant or powerful group live an idealistic existence, never straying too far from the norms of their culture. They never realize that they are in a bubble of sorts—a magic circle. They *know* what is real and are confident in this knowledge. It takes one who has been expelled from this privileged place, like Virginia Foster Durr in her autobiography, to talk about being outside the magic circle.

I chose willingly to step outside of my circle. I was a minority who grew up in what would be considered by all standards a poor neighborhood. I, however, was smart and liked school. I was able to leave that neighborhood and become a college professor. I had a prominent career and was able to retire with honors. Over the years, I had been the principal investigator on numerous multimillion-dollar projects. I was a respected member of my community. I had money in the bank and investments and was ready to have an eventful and fun retirement.

It was at this time in my life that I decided to take on a great responsibility. I am a mother and never thought I would be free of parental duties, but after many years, I was. Both of my sons are grown by legal and cultural standards.

Now, in my sixties, I had agreed to take on the care of a teenaged granddaughter. Just entering her fourteenth year, she had been deemed a juvenile by the courts. Bringing up children as a minority parent can be very dicey. Everything is relative or so it seemed. How do you teach right from wrong when the child can clearly see how ambivalent the culture can be? I was beginning to fear the future. I was entering unfamiliar territory, but I had had experiences with the criminal justice system, so I thought I knew what to expect.

I was born in a small Southern city of about 30,000 people. It is a blue-collar town known for Pullman Standard cars, steel mills, and any other dirty and dangerous job you could think of. I am a minority in America, so I know about dirty and dangerous. I hated my hometown. It was a dangerous, nefarious place. The part of town that you lived in meant you could not easily move into anyone else's territory. Even dating a guy from another part of town could create an incident. He might get run out of the neighborhood if he was fast or beaten up by the neighborhood gangs if he was slow.

Being a minority, especially black, when I was a kid, meant you had to navigate everything, from the simplest act to a complex negotiation. Each of these triangulations was necessary to stay out of trouble. Staying out of trouble was important if you were going to reach your goals. I was goal-oriented, so staying out of trouble was a necessity for me. The journey to adulthood taught me that it was not easy for everyone.

I saw friends and family become victims, repeatedly. Staying out of trouble was complex and difficult. Most were not able to do it successfully. Somewhere along the line, there was going to be trouble. White Americans mostly live in the magic circle. They do not know this other world, the nefarious one. Furthermore, they do not want to know that it exists either. My uncle, who lived in Chicago, Illinois, once said, "You are going to get shaken down by the police in Chicago, the thing is not if, but when."

Generally, they do not bother whites; they do not know who they are related to or how. They would shake them down too if it were not more of a risk for them. Shaking a black person down has few risks. We do not have powerful families. We do not have powerful connections. We are just ripe for the pickings. There is, however, an underground world. We could be some powerful person's outside child. We could be connected to the powerful in all sorts of weird ways, but the risk is still low. Someone will always be willing to take that risk for gain.

As I have grown older, I have come to appreciate my hometown. You could not just get by on your looks there. You had to have skills. We learned to cultivate those skills. We were good at surviving. Give us a loaf of bread, some sugar, mayonnaise, and ketchup, and we have a meal for several days. What, you never had a mayo, sugar, or ketchup sandwich? Nothing is better when you are hungry in the summer. Wait, do not forget the Kool-Aid.

Oh, blacks are just paranoid, you might say. Well, just about every regular black person that I know, male or female, has had some incident with the police. Now, if you are a rich black person, you can live in a cocoon. You can avoid contact with the unpleasant side of life. You can avoid public transportation and most of the hassles of life. You can shop where you are treated with dignity. You can interact with like-minded people and avoid unpleasantness. But even the well-off, like me, are often faced with unpleasantness.

For example, when I was in my fifties, three friends and I became rabid antique buyers. Some of us were so hooked that we had additional public storage sheds in which to keep our treasures. One night, after a particularly fruitful auction, we had purchased more items than we wanted to take home. In anticipation of this wonderful night, we rented a U-Haul to hold these goodies.

We had stopped by the storage area to drop off our purchases when a police car stopped. An officer got out and asked us what we were doing. We explained that we were dropping off furniture purchased at an auction. He indicated that there was an *all-points bulletin* out for persons in a U-Haul who had burglarized students' apartments on the university's campus. Now, I was a faculty member on the campus, another woman was a faculty member at a college in town, and the other was a nurse practitioner with her own women's center. The other friend across the street, watching all of this unfold, was also a faculty member at the university.

He asked for permission and received it to look at the furniture. As he perused our purchases—namely, a couple of winged back chairs and several Duncan Phyfe tables and sofas—he remarked that none of these items would have been in a college student's apartment. After a slightly nervous laugh, he said that we could go. We were furious, but we kept our cool and asked for his name. One friend intended to report him and did. We never heard anything or got a response.

As we were leaving, he remarked that the bulletin about the description of the U-Haul had not matched ours but he felt the need to check it out anyway. Why were we in need of checking out? What was suspicious about forty- to fifty-year-old black women at a storage facility at night? Was it that it was night? Did we look like *cat burglars?* Would he have checked out three white forty- to fifty-year-old women?

My answer is no. Even today, black women are routinely humiliated. If you challenge the system, you will pay a price. Just recently, Faya Rose Toure, a prominent attorney in Selma, Alabama, was violated for peacefully protesting in support of an increase in Medicaid payments and the Black Lives Matter movement. Protestors were spray-painting the sidewalks and streets, but at that time, Attorney Toure had not spray-painted anything. She simply asked why another protestor was being arrested. While peacefully protesting, asking a simple question can get you arrested.

Getting arrested was just the beginning of the ordeal for Toure. She was treated in an inhumane manner with a forced walk upstairs and handcuffed from behind. The final humiliation was being stripped searched and forced to cough three times while jailers observed her naked backside for contraband. The other female protestor received a similar fate, but the male protestors were not stripped searched. This is America in the twenty-first century.

Introduction

I am putting this book together for those who have unfortunately entered the *nefarious zone*. Please understand that this is not an indictment against the culture. It does what it is intended to do. When you find yourself in the zone, you are already condemned by the system. You have allowed yourself or someone close to you to be found in a compromising situation. You have been deemed to be unworthy because of this. First, you are automatically viewed as a *bad* mother, father, or person. While you are in the zone, this status is rarely able to be changed. Just know that this is how you are viewed and you will have to make the best of it. I found myself in the nefarious zone and have stories to share that may be helpful in digging your way out.

    I am an adult with no criminal violations, only a few traffic violations. I have never been accused of a crime other than speeding. At least once I was caught in a speed trap. One beautiful Sunday morning while driving to church, I drove down a steep hill at more than twenty-five miles an hour. I pled guilty and took the driving online course for $150.

    I tried to fight it and went to court with displays and everything. I testified that it was impossible to come down that hill and maintain twenty-five miles per hour without riding your brakes. The judge said, "Well, ride your brakes next time." Although I am the slowest driver that I know, I changed my plea and accepted my fate. Even my mother drove faster than me.

I am using my experiences, both failures and successes, to help you navigate the nefarious zone. While going through similar issues, I came to know and work with an entire community. I journeyed through and now am mostly past the difficult parts. You can do the same. You can manage within the system, but here are a few lessons learned.

Because I feel the need to address these problems, I do not want to violate the privacy of family or friends. I have included names only when given permission to do so. Everything that I report here happened but maybe not in the manner reported. I have included the experiences of many but changed who and what was involved. I have learned much and want to share. Greater power is involved, I do believe. So follow what I say with that in mind.

First, do you have spiritual underpinnings? You are going to need a force greater than yourself. Whether that be Jehovah, Yahweh, Lord, Jesus, Buddha, or some other spirit, call on them. If you get no response, then call on another higher spirit. Ask for guidance.

If you do not believe in anything greater than yourself, then just look up at the sky at night. We are just a speck of dust in the universe. How, what, and who are all unknowns. I believe in a higher power, but I do not dismiss those who do not. You must find a way to do the same things with less mental comfort. I believe in the ultimate power of right and wrong. I do not necessarily think it resides in the work of *man,* though. Man, *male and female,* created culture and the relative right or wrong depending on who is in power. I believe in spiritual right or wrong. Later, I will discuss these views in greater detail in another section.

I have a prayer box in which I place my prayers. You might have a meditation box in which you place your desires and wants. My good friend Dorothy heard about this prayer box called the *God* box from a spokesperson on one of those TV shopping networks. You write what you want to give over to God or your greater self and place it in the box. They have these boxes in stores, or you can make your own from a shoebox or any gift box. The point is that you pray and give it over to God. If you are still worried, go and get it out of the box. You do not trust in God to handle it, so work it out yourself. I have taken very few things out of the box lately. I am much more relaxed and less stressed.

One night, Dorothy and I were discussing the God box, and she remarked that she had more prayers for me and my family in her box than she had for herself and her family. She was taking the prayers for me out because most of them had been affirmatively answered. I was surprised to review these prayers and, much to my surprise, I found that they had been answered.

The daughter of my new community friend had gotten into trouble with the undercover narcotics guys. They had charged her with drug possession. They wanted her to roll over on the big guys to get out of legal trouble herself. Even I could see that this could get her killed. You cannot go to the bathroom in this city without someone knowing when and what you did. You just go to jail for your crimes. Who is going to protect you from these drug dealers? We had to pray for her. So far, even though fired upon and having to run through the woods, she is still alive.

This brings us to the next thing you should know. Do you have *street credibility?* Better known in the streets as *creds*. I was fortunate that I had grown up in what is now called the *hood* and learned something about the streets as a child. I, however, had left that world over fifty years ago and had not looked back. I had to learn that world again. If I was going to communicate with my young people, I had to understand why they did the things they did. They do not trust you to navigate the street world. I do not blame them for that. I did not live in that world, but I had to get up to speed and fast.

The criminal justice system is based on rewards and punishments. It is designed to work on normal children who get into trouble because they are hanging out with *bad* children. If your child is this type of child, then the criminal justice system will *scare the crap* out of them and they will stay clear of it. If this is you, then pass this book on to someone who has a more serious problem.

If your child is not normal and is guided by the street culture, you are in trouble and need all the love and help you can get. If your child is the *bad* child, then you are living the street life whether you live in a million-dollar mansion or a $500-a-month subsidized apartment. Your child is a product of the streets. It is easy to have this type of child today.

Let us be perfectly honest. Street life is glorified. Our children listen to music and are captivated by the internet that streams 24/7. Start listening to what your child hears and views, and then turn off the websites they use. You can simply ask or go on YouTube or look up the sites on their phones. If you do not know what to ask, ask the police because they keep up with it all. They monitor the major sites. Young people are always ahead of the game, so be vigilant.

Last, know your child. Is your child *normal?* What are you dealing with here? Did your child just get into trouble or has there been a long-standing problem? Has your child had serious trauma? Are drugs involved? Do you really know your child? If not, you better get with it and fast. Is your child suicidal or likely to hurt themselves in some way?

Remember, the criminal justice system is based on rewards and punishments. If children are doing more to hurt themselves than the system might do, then you are in trouble. Punishment does not mean the same thing to them. They might like pain. If you discover this, then you need help from professionals. Just know that you cannot force your child to get help, and sometimes they are smarter than the professionals. I pray for you because it is going to be a long journey for you.

Chapter 1

Spiritual Underpinnings

This chapter can be omitted by anyone who finds that it is not useful to them in understanding and navigating their problems. You may find the other chapters more useful and to the point, but if you need spiritual help, use this chapter. The first thing you will find when you get involved in a serious problem is that people will start challenging your actions. Before the problem, you were a reasonable person whose opinion was valued highly. Now, you are suspect. Everyone will start questioning your actions and decisions. Every decision that you make will be challenged. You need to do something other than what you are suggesting. This would be fine if, when you asked "What would you do?" then challengers tend to come up with generalities. For example, you need to be firmer, you need to practice tough love, or you give them too much. When you ask how they would practice this, no one has an answer.

To put it succinctly, the bottom line is you need to enter this situation as if you are going into battle. You need to be fortified. I entered the nefarious zone using Bible verses and biblical self-help books. You can find them everywhere. When a judge told me that I had nothing to say that she wanted to hear and that perhaps I was the one who had abused my granddaughter, I was stunned. I was a retired college professor with over thirty years of work experience. If she had read anything about the case or had knowledge of the case, she would have known that I had not had any contact with the granddaughter for fourteen years. She literally cursed me out in a very judgelike way.

I had no standing with the court. The power of attorney that I had was not worth the paper it was written on. Unless you have custody, no one wants to hear from you. You find that you have few friends and little support. If you can identify a friend, try to cultivate that friendship. You will need friends and support, so you need to keep calm and not argue with anyone. How I kept my center intact was to use verses from the New International version of the Holy Bible. I had two favorites. I read Proverbs and 1 Corinthians often. You might find your favorites.

Then I used specific verses that related to what I was feeling. There are many books that address the specific needs of the reader. For instance, if you are feeling anxious, what verses address that emotion? These books use verses to help you deal with your condition. I have tried to capture the feelings that I had at the time and the verses that helped me. Remember, this is just a guide and not anything that must be taken as the be all or end all. Be flexible here and take what you need. I feel for what you are going through because I have been there. You need love and understanding, and you will get little in the way of either.

The first emotion that I remember feeling was confusion. I was second-guessing my decisions. Was I doing the right thing? What I mean by this is "Was I interacting with my granddaughter in an appropriate manner?" Several friends remarked that they would not accept the type of behavior that I was experiencing. They remarked that they would just have to let her go. Several times I asked, what does that mean? How do you let a fifteen-year-old go?

You must have confidence in the decisions you make, and you will get very little support when you decide on a course of action. You must have faith that you are making the appropriate decisions. If you do not trust your decisions, you are doomed. I felt an immense feeling of confidence in my decisions when I prayed about them.

I often asked for a *sign* that I was doing the right thing. Generally, I felt a sense of well-being when I was making the *right* decision. What is a sign? I can just say that you know when you are receiving a sign.

One day I asked for a sign and a red bird flew onto my porch and looked directly into my eyes. I decided that was a sign. I may have been mistaken, but I took it as a sign. It turned out to be a good sign because it moved me in a positive direction.

Prayer

I am a highly educated person and, if childhood IQ tests are believable, I am also above average in intelligence. Yet I was so inadequate in navigating the justice system. I questioned everything. I became tentative and a second-guesser. I worried about every simple decision. My family and friends suggested that I pray more.

This is when I had to ask myself some really hard questions. Did I really believe in prayer? Was there something metaphysical working with prayer? Did we simply imagine that prayer worked? I prayed, but did I really pray? I decided to start with just a conversation. For every decision I had to make, I asked for guidance and a sign that I was moving in the right direction. I made the *God box* (a box into which you place your prayers). I put my prayers in written form. All my questions and prayers I put into this box. Immediately, a weight was lifted off my shoulders. I kid you not, I sometimes had my answer the next day. What were the signs? Well, I felt confident about my decisions. Often, I woke with a joyful feeling. I cannot remember when I felt joyful. I took these feelings as my signs. You may ask what were my questions. Well, I will discuss them in the later chapters. I do not want to get into specifics here. I just want to focus on my feelings around these questions.

Use family and friends and, most of all, prayers to deal with the frustrations, anxieties, and confusion you have in life. It does not matter what the questions or problems. Just deal with your feelings. All will be handled. A prayer that I found helpful is 1 Peter 5:10–11 (NIV), "And the God of grace, who called you to his eternal glory in Christ, after you have suffered a little while, will himself restore you and make you strong, firm, and steadfast. To him be the power for ever and ever.

Amen." In Joshua 1:9 (NIV), it says, "Have I not commanded you? Be strong and courageous. Do not be afraid; do not be discouraged, for the Lord your God will be with you wherever you go."

I did not realize that I had received many blessings and that my prayers had been answered until my best friend Dorothy started taking prayers out of her box. She talked about how many of my prayers had been answered. When I realized that my prayers had been answered, I remembered one of my favorite Bible parables, the story of Jesus healing the ten men with leprosy in Luke 17:11–19 (NIV). Ten were healed, but only one returned, praising God in a loud voice. He was a Samaritan, and he threw himself at Jesus and thanked him. I started to be more thankful and began to feel gratitude for each small success that I had.

The Old and Primitive Brain

I did not realize how important what you thought could have been in how you behaved. Since I have worked in the research and academic world for over fifty years, I know that this is difficult to believe, but I had a simplistic view of the way that people behaved. I had worked for fifteen years with medical researchers and realized early on that many of our clients had a simplistic view of the world and did not trust doctors or science. I did not realize that I also had such a view. I was shocked to find that I was guided by views that were archaic. For example, I really believed that if you heard something many times that it must be true. I realized that psychologically this was one of the reasons that advertisements work. Our parents knew that this worked, so they repeated things thousands of times over the course of our childhood.

I, however, felt repetition in child-rearing was unnecessary because you would simply bore the child to death. My simplistic view was that you tell the child something once or twice, and they would eventually learn. I did not understand that it was important to make this action almost like breathing. I did not realize that my view was far too simplistic. I thought that my thinking was better and more modern in its scope. I had not considered the old brain. The old brain functions to regulate basic survival, like breathing, moving, resting, feeding, and emotion. The old brain, known as the stem, is the oldest and innermost part of the brain.

The old brain is wired to maintain our survival. When we deal with difficult situations, we are not dealing with the intelligent brain. We are dealing with the old brain. We do not talk much about the old brain, but it is there and ready to take control during a crisis. So, what do spiritual underpinnings have to do with the old brain? The old brain is instinctual and it operates without much thought. Our spiritual underpinnings must function with the old brain. When the young man with encephalitis was functioning in a normal fashion, he was praying. He knew something was wrong but he did not know what, so he prayed.

I found out about the old brain and how it functions from two sources—first when my friend's son contracted encephalitis, and later when I had a stroke that attacked the old brain. I could reason well, but I had trouble placing numbers in the correct order. Frankly, we do not think much about the old brain. We live in the twenty-first century, in the age of computers, smartphones, and the internet. Yet the old brain is there and waiting. It likes repetition; it likes chaos, and that is how it functions. There is fight and flight. It does not matter what we teach that is reasonable. In the end, it will function at the basic level.

Get into trouble and you are functioning on a primitive level. I say that I viewed everything simplistically. I was informed by the police that jail is the only place where you can put some people with brain injuries. They can be dangerous, so you lock them up. They cannot be controlled and drugs do not always work on them. There are limited numbers of beds for these wounded individuals, so many find themselves locked up behind bars.

I thought we could teach ourselves to be reasonable, but no. We are not reasonable when we are under stress. We are in the primitive zone. We will either fight you or run from you. So, when I had to communicate, I started screaming my response rather than talking in a reasonable tone. This usually jolts the person out of the old brain mode. Then I started the reasonable discussion. How did I figure this out? It came to me in a dream one night. I remembered how my discussions with family usually went. I am not talking about abuse here. I am talking about a strategy that must be used when you are fully conscious of your motives. You must get the person to hear you.

You are not immune to the impact of the old brain. When you are stressed, you are functioning at a primitive level as well. So, preparing for battle is key to your success. Every morning I got up and prepared for battle by praying and meditating about my day. I did not do this every morning, but I tried to do this every day. Things happen in life, but I tried to maintain a pattern of behavior with prayer at the center.

Chapter 2

Understanding the Nefarious Zone

After you have prepared yourself for a long, retracted spiritual struggle, then you need to understand where you are. First, what is your background? What experiences can you rely on to help you? Are you completely clueless? You must understand that in most nefarious zones you will have to have some credibility to function. I was born in a nefarious zone so I had some knowledge. I, however, had not lived in that zone for many years. How had things changed? I had no idea. I still had friends and family who lived in the zone, and I needed to find out more from them. So began the journey to find out more about the zone in which I found myself.

This is the discovery phase. I will discuss the journey of several people. To maintain the confidentiality of our participants, I have combined the factual information into one or two stories. The nefarious zone is the criminal justice system. I am sure that the intentions of the persons who put this zone together were not what eventually became the outcome, but you must work with what you have. Now, the very first experience that one of our participants had is to discover that in this zone there is no such thing as *confidentiality*. One participant had a child who had experienced some form of trafficking. We are not sure what was involved because the child refused to discuss the experience. You will find that this is *commonplace*. You will never have the full picture. You will have bits and pieces that you need to put together, like a puzzle.

One day, the participant was alone with her daughter's boyfriend, while the daughter was getting dressed for their date, when he asked her a question. He had been locked up in the juvenile facility in the town where they lived. You will find that this is common. Your young person will find people in similar situations to be more accepting. The *bad* stick together because they are more comfortable with each other. He asked, "What is trafficking?" This person was surprised to learn that he knew about the term. She asked how he knew the word. He said that one of the juvenile officers had asked him who was his girlfriend, and when he told him, the officer had said, "Stay away from her. She was trafficked."

Since he already had damaging information, she decided to be open with him. She said that some bad things had happened to her daughter and she did not want it discussed in her town. Could he please not repeat the information that he had learned? He agreed, and she proceeded to tell him what she knew about trafficking. This was many years ago, and she feels that he never repeated the information to anyone. He was better about keeping the confidential information than the person charged with his job to do so.

Well, when you discover that there is a problem like this, what do you do? People who have not had experiences in the nefarious zone will report it. Now, those of us who have had experiences will be reluctant to report it. First, the officer's job could be in jeopardy. What will the system protect first, a damaged and possibly trafficked girl or a man's livelihood? We believed in the livelihood, so it was not reported. Was this the right decision? We may never know for sure, but these are the decisions that you will have to routinely make in the nefarious zone, so you should have some strategy in mind to help you make them. What will help you have the best outcome? You need to have a strategy that outlines the goals and objectives in your plan to understand and navigate the zone.

The guides that I used were from the book *The Art of War* or, as it is referred to, *Sun Tzu* and the principles of Ma'at. I have several versions of *Sun Tzu*, but the translation I like the best is the Denma one. In my research and academic work, I have often applied the wisdom of these works. There is a debate about the origins and indeed whether the author of the work, Sun Tzu, even existed. *The Art of War* is reputed to have been compiled about 2,300 years ago in what is now north China and represents the collective thinking of warriors in conflict. Ancient thought like Ma'at is also controversial, but the application of this thinking has been useful to me in my work in the health field. It has helped me understand why people do the things that they do. I found it to be a helpful guide in my profession, so I used it as I tried to navigate the nefarious zone.

The major tenet of *The Art of War* is represented here:

> One hundred victories in one hundred
> battles in not the most skillful.
> Subduing the other's military without
> battle is the most skillful.

I liked this book because no matter the experiences, the wisdom of the work is available to everyone. It is useful as a guide, but it does not have to be slavishly followed. It provides guidance and a model of behavior that will help you gain insight into its teachings. *Sun Tzu* proposes that conflict is a central component of life. It is the foundation of our lives. If we recall the discussion of the old brain, conflict is central to our survival, but when not controlled can end our lives.

Sun Tzu proposes that our response to conflict begins with knowledge of ourselves and others. In chapter 3 of *The Art of War*:
And so, in the military—

> Knowing the other and knowing oneself,

In one hundred battles no danger.
Not knowing the other and knowing oneself.
One victory for one loss.

> Not knowing the other and not knowing oneself.
> In every battle certain defeat.

In trying to understand the nefarious zone, I have gone back to the ancient knowledge of African and Asian scholars. I found this knowledge to be most helpful in my journey. I recommend that you try to find what is most helpful to you. Hopefully, this guide will assist you along the way. In the nefarious zone, four major issues are interrelated: the old brain, spiritual health, mental health, and a problematic area. Although I have focused on the zone, it is simply part of a larger whole. The whole has many interrelated and moving parts. All things are interconnected. No wonder we get lost trying to navigate this ever-changing world.

Yet we have a set of shared assumptions about how things work. Different schools of thought emphasize different aspects. I decided to use the general school of thought proposed by ancient Africa and Asia. I do not offer them as perfect but rather as some of the oldest and most well-tested schools of thought. The basic assumption here is that the world is in constant flow or flux. The rulers are powerful because they are at the head of a complex set of relationships. These relationships contrast with the personal which are defined by strength, morality, and ability. These personal qualities belong to an individual, not necessarily to the leaders or, in fact, the world.

So a leader is not necessarily moral or strong but could be. The leader is powerful because of the position that he or she occupies within the larger whole, not because of the personal qualities possessed. This position may be based on ancestry, virtue, physical strength, and other qualities, but the current holder need not have any of these qualities personally. The leader may have gained power by immoral or amoral means. The leader may have manipulated the environment to achieve goals that are not admirable or valued by the culture, but once in power, that person is able to wield power through the manipulation of the complex set of relationships. This is difficult for most of us to accept.

A judge in the criminal justice system, for example, could be immoral or amoral, but still powerful within that position.

The advantage that we have as individuals has to do with the qualities of the world. The world is cohesive. The leader is in a position that was not created in a vacuum. The leader is only powerful when conjoined with larger patterns of influence. These patterns of influence usually support the leader because they understand that when they do not, this may allow others to use the environment to evidence change to their advantage. The term *shih* is a function of the relationship among things.

Originally, shih was the power of the leader to control others or affect them from a distance. Soon, the subjects of the leader understood that the power did not reside in the person of the leader, but rather in the position occupied by that leader. You, however, have the power to make changes to the environment that might work to your advantage. You may not have the personal qualities that your culture values or the power base necessary to make changes. You, however, may know someone who has power, or you may be able to use the qualities of others, such as a legislator, pastor, teacher, or public official to make a change. Shih is a function of the relationship among these things. It is dependent on how things are arranged to interconnect.

How do we learn to master shih? Three major ways are emphasized in *Sun Tzu*. First, short phrases are used to summarize complex arguments. Second, the text teaches by metaphor and image. Third, shih is illustrated by giving examples of it. Here is an illustration of how I used shih to understand more about how the nefarious zone worked.

Let me get this out of the way right now. I am prejudiced against the criminal justice system. I am a minority who grew up in the segregated South of the mid-twentieth century. I was a victim of this system. It was created to track me down and return me as a fugitive slave, even after slavery was de facto abolished. Given that most of this was done during a very stressful time, I surmise that the old brain was the dominant brain. The police would just as soon shoot me as breathe. It was like survival mode for both the hunter and the hunted.

So my first contact with the court was when my grandchild was accused of theft and there was a preliminary hearing to determine how to proceed. It is at this time that the judge told me to *shut up* because the power of attorney that I had was not worth the paper it was written on. My son was the legal guardian and was not present because of the demands of his job. The judge was furious and took it out on me. She yelled and demeaned me for almost thirty minutes. She even accused me of possibly abusing my granddaughter during this time. Now my academic training was helpful, but I wanted to hurt her. I felt that her demeaning manner made me look weak and ineffective before my granddaughter. The lack of respect from the court was troublesome because my granddaughter felt she needed to defend my honor.

What in effect happened here was a good example of what happens to many participants in court. To begin, you are in a court so already you are suspect. You are quickly sized up as unworthy of respect and attention. To the judge, I was an incompetent woman wasting her time. I, however, felt quite differently. I wanted her to understand that I had taken this on not to waste her time but to try and protect my granddaughter from herself and her destructive behavior. I had been blindsided by this action of theft. She had been doing *A and B* work in school. Everything was going well, and then this happened.

Now let us examine the shih. If I lashed out at the judge, I would be legally liable and possibly would have to pay a fine or spend time in jail. I came into court feeling hopeful, but soon like harmless water, I was propelled into a river where I could drown. The water had become deadly. Many people drown in fast-moving streams of water when the harmless water becomes a raging torrent.

I looked around the courtroom and saw the eyes of people who seemed to feel sorry for my treatment, but no one said a word. The judge was in a powerful position, and the only help would have come from my granddaughter, who wanted to fight the judge. I said that I was fine but challenged myself to stop saying things I did not mean. No, I was not fine. I wanted to hurt somebody. I was humiliated so I acknowledged this. This was somewhat of a breakthrough because I was able to explain how I felt, but I was able to refrain from causing more harm by getting control of myself and not acting out. I was able to model the behavior that I wanted my granddaughter to emulate.

I looked over at the district attorney who seemed to be saying with her eyes that she understood. I took this as a sign to approach her later. The judge ruled that the hearing would be postponed until my son could be present. After the hearing, I approached the district attorney, and she gave me a mental health care provider's name and card. She felt that I might get help for the granddaughter. I wanted to hurt the judge, but I used my energy to make positive contact and get help for the mental health issues that we had.

Chapter 3

Know Yourself and Others

As stated by Sun Tzu, if you do not know yourself and the other, then defeat will be yours. Knowing yourself is perhaps easier than you think. We have a good idea of who we are, and it should come as no surprise that we are complicated. What may be a surprise is just how complicated we are, and how that plays into the decisions that we make in the nefarious zone. There are many books on how to determine your personality and many of them are free. You can also have your personality professionally evaluated. There are psychometrists in larger communities and many have alliances with the local school systems. For a small fee, you can get your personality assessed, but for our purposes, you can do your own.

The test is not very complicated and you can use a version of one of the most popular, the Myers-Briggs Personality Test. Most personality evaluation tools use some aspects of the Myers-Briggs. The test does not need to be taken too seriously. It is a general guide to self. You already know a great deal about self, but you may be unsure how to evaluate what is important and needs to be addressed. The Myers-Briggs test breaks personality down into sixteen distinct types. These distinct personality types are useful, but you do not have to have these distinctive breakdowns. A general idea of the most important components is all that you will usually need. I prefer to defer to professionals when I need detailed information. So I focused on the general personality traits.

If you examine the general personality traits, you can see if you are extrovert versus introvert, optimist versus pessimist, victor versus victim, confident versus anxious, and morning versus evening. Few are ever totally any one trait but a combination that leans to one or another extreme. Then personalities can be rated based on the willingness to take risks, how confident a person is, how trustworthy, honest, altruistic, and ambitious, and how healthy and happy you are with yourself and your body. How well you communicate and the relationships you have with family, friends, and partners are important variants of personality. Then there is your reasoning and logical thinking, and your work skills and the work environment. There are other miscellaneous characteristics, such as your daily habits, including shopping, being mature, and feeling entitled.

In the nefarious zone, reasoning, logical thinking ability, and honesty are perhaps of paramount importance. It is here that the rubber hits the road. What is your street credibility? Since the nefarious zone is characterized by evil, then the perception that you are honest may make it appear that you are or will become a victim and weak. Being honest and trustworthy is not as valuable as knowing the way around the system's rules and regulations. You might think that you are being honest when in fact you may simply be acting in a naïve manner. The court system will make you look like you are incompetent if you are not knowledgeable. Being innocent is not as important as being able to prove your innocence. You need to prove everything, so forget about whether you are innocent and focus on how to prove it.

The key is finding out how you think and how that affects the way others think. Getting results can be as important as being innocent of the offense. I found out that it might be better to let the person stay in jail until the trial since this gives the impression that you are taking the offense seriously. In many instances, parents and friends are viewed as enablers and coddlers of the *bad* person. If you let the person experience some of the consequences of bad behavior, the justice system views this positively. So if you are afraid to let the person have some hard knocks, you will be viewed as *soft* on crime. Trying to view the offense seriously and not trying to explain or defend the offender's behavior is particularly important.

You are thought of as an enabler so your attempts to explain and defend the offender will not be viewed as positive. You view yourself as truthful and honest, but that may not be the way you are viewed in the nefarious zone. Remember, evil and bad behavior is paramount, so everyone is viewed with suspicion.

Also, being truthful and honest is more difficult than you think. How many times have you let people you care about see you do something dishonest? Whether it be cheating on your income tax and getting into a movie theater or club with a fake id, how many times have you violated some rule? When someone is caught being dishonest, is your concern that they got caught or that they did something dishonest? You must *get real* here. What is your real concern? Remember, people are watching you. You are a role model for the offender. They will see everything that you do and will call you on every dishonest behavior.

Why must you be concerned? First, if you are praying for help, you need to be upfront. I do not believe that you can pray and continue to be a liar and dishonest. Maybe you feel that you can, but I think not. Who are you fooling? If you put on the armor of God and you are dishonest, will this work out well for you? I know of a participant who would not let her son stay in jail until the trial. She got him out on bail when she knew he was still drinking and using. When it came time for him to report to a rehab facility for treatment after receiving probation, she swore that he had been with her the whole time and was not drinking or taking drugs. The treatment center did not take her word and tested him on the spot. He had been using and the facility would not take him. He had to go back to jail.

Now, one of the strategies used was to keep him in jail until he could get the treatment needed before he could drink again. She did not have the faith to leave him in jail until that happened. One of the reasons was the court kept delaying his release. No one is going to make it easy for you to function in the nefarious zone. Nothing is going to work out well for you. You must have faith and be strong. You must know yourself and the others.

You do not believe that drug addicts will violate a chance to receive treatment but they will. They may not be thinking in a logical or reasonable way. They are drug addicts. This is your precious child and it is difficult to believe, but your child is probably a stone-cold addict. Later that year, the child got out but was still an addict and is to this day.

Now, terrible things happen in jail and this participant was afraid that bad things would happen to her son. But you are in the nefarious zone and bad things are more likely to happen. You must be able to function and take calculated risks to save the offender, a family member or a friend. People get raped in jail. There is access to drugs in jail, but less than on the outside. The problem is one of likelihood. You are more likely to be harmed if you succumb to your own fears. Your fears may be even more realized depending on the characteristics of the other—your child, friend, or other family members.

Who are they? One of the participants told the story of a young person who was accused of having stolen from the elderly. This is viewed as a particularly heinous crime, and the seriousness is viewed, in the fact, as a higher-level felony. She told the parent that she had been stealing since she was six years old. She had been brought up by a criminal gang and theft was a way of life for her.

You can see very clearly that you are dealing with different issues when a teenager has been stealing since childhood. You are dealing with a more difficult problem. You are not only dealing with the criminal offense but the ingrained behavior of the person. You can, however, work to reeducate the person, but this is a long-term issue that will take many years past the nefarious zone experience to reconcile.

Then there are the extremely problematic issues. For example, does the offender have a borderline personality disorder? I am not telling you to try and handle these issues by yourself. You will need professional help, but please understand that the success rate with these disorders is low. If you have the interaction of being in the criminal justice system and borderline personality disorder, you are indeed deeply in the nefarious zone. These disorders occur in childhood when our personalities are formed. Something goes wrong and the person suffers trauma for years. These can be life-long issues, so be prepared for the long haul.

According to the Mayo Clinic's website, a borderline personality disorder is a mental health disorder that impacts the manner of thinking and feeling about the self and others. This thinking causes problems in everyday life functioning. This includes self-image issues and difficulty in managing emotions and behavior. This results in a pattern of unstable relationships with others. Anger issues and impulsive and frequent mood swings are major characteristics of the disorder.

If the person is fantasizing or has mental images about hurting self or suicidal thoughts, take emergency action and call 911 or call the National Suicide Prevention Lifeline at 1-800-273-TALK or 1-800-273-8255 any time, day or night, and push "1" to be put in touch with the Veterans Crisis Line. You might find it helpful to contact a mental health provider, a loved one, or someone from the faith community. You know the person so you may have to choose the best prevention mode. Remember that when you call 911 that the police are coming, so be prepared to navigate the situation which could quickly escalate.

For those offenders who have a borderline personality disorder but are not thinking about hurting themselves, check out the internet for a summary of this disorder, www.mind-diagnostic.org/free. The disorder is characterized by unstable moods, behavior, and overall functioning. According to the internet, the disorder is common with more than three million cases per year. Symptoms vary from person to person, but common symptoms include the following: distorted self-image; feelings of isolation, boredom, and emptiness; sometimes severe and sudden mood swings; feelings of anxiety; suicidal thoughts, delusions; and loss of interest in routine activities.

Other complications may include repeated job losses and changes, drop-outs, conflict-riddled relationships, abusive relationships, self-injury, unplanned pregnancies, sexually-transmitted infections, vehicular accidents, and other impulsive and risky behavior. As you can see, the interaction between these serious symptoms and the old brain can be catastrophic. You are over your head here, but you can still find a path to healing. Try to learn as much as you can so you can pass this on to professional help. Remember, this can be a time-saver. The person with the personality disorder may be difficult to treat, but you have an advantage in that the person may trust you. You can help facilitate the treatment by giving the therapist information that may take them years to get from the offender.

In addition, the person may have other mental health issues, such as depression; alcohol and substance abuse issues; anxiety, eating, and bipolar disorders; post-traumatic stress disorder (PTSD); attention-deficit/hyperactivity disorder (ADHD); and other personality disorders. It can be overwhelming for anyone, much less the family member or friend entering the zone unaware of what is before them. One person deemed entering the zone is like living dog years. In other words, for each normal year, you live five to seven years. It is no wonder that after a stressful period, people look visibly older.

Chapter 4

Challenges, Surprises, and Lessons Learned

The journey has provided many surprises and lessons. The outline of these lessons has helped provide a framework for a strategy to motivate change in my community. After five person-years and twenty-five presidential years, I have formed what I see as basic notions about change. What are presidential years, you might ask? Well, if you remember, I spoke of them earlier in this book as dog years. When President Kennedy was assassinated, I was in my high school English class and my teacher, Mrs. Cunningham, relayed the horrible news to us. She said that the job of president of the United States of America was incredibly stressful. She pointed to a photo of Kennedy on our bulletin board before he was president and there was a very youthful image, and then she pointed to a recent photo that showed a much older man. "See, presidents live five years to our one," she remarked. After about three years, our president was visibly older, about ten to fifteen years older. I never forgot that moment. I guess everyone who experienced that day felt that way.

Quite surprisingly, the journey has led to an attempt to break down the code of silence around the criminal justice system. I have examined and tried to help formulate a strategy to deal with the personal trials of being a young person in the criminal justice system. I tried to explain how many in the system have multiple personality and behavior problems that need addressing. Sitting by and watching allows discriminatory behavior to play out, proceed, and continue. If we are to believe what we hear, *that a few bad apples have contaminated the barrel,* then we need to take out the bad apples. Is this not what the communities are saying as well? Many communities with bad reputations are sounding the alarm that they are being victimized too. What is the truth? Which versions are we experiencing?

First, I was shocked to learn that much of the framework of my interdisciplinary work is based on theories that I had learned in the early 1970s. The outline of these lessons helped provide a framework for a strategy to motivate change in our communities. The first lesson learned is that *truth* for many is what has been told to us by those we trust. Even seemingly ridiculous things are believed if passed on by a trusted person.

On the other hand, if we do not trust you, you are perceived as dangerous. These dangerous people are never the people in our circle. We do not go to school with them. We do not see them in church. They do not live in our neighborhoods. If they are seen as not trustworthy, then they do not possess the qualities that are viewed as *truthful*. So, we must find something that is trustworthy; something that lives outside of our personal community. The notion of the *beloved community* immediately came to mind as the concept that could serve as a starting point. I frankly never believed in it as a viable goal. We are too flawed as a people to ever come together as a beloved community. When I thought about it, however, I realized one important fact. Very few people are bold enough to view and act as if their bad behavior is acceptable.

Even when we kill someone, we like to make it appear justifiable. In every case, the bad try to make their bad behavior seem good. The starting point then must be to create what has been described as a place where truth and justice are real. I have several friends who have devoted their lives to trying to create these changes in our world. I always saw their work as needed but realistically as not attainable to those they trained.

Interestingly, the people who do the work to help us be our better selves seem to come from similar perspectives. One such group is

VISIONS, Inc. With roots going back into our ancient past, VISIONS, Inc. and others were formulated from the work of the Southeast Institute for Group and Family Therapy. The Southeast Institute offers psychotherapy services and continuing education workshops for mental health professionals. Based on the notion of our three egos—parent, adult, and the child—and giving a nod to an African-centered view of the world that encompassed Pan-Africanism and the Civil Rights Movement, VISIONS, Inc. is the organization whose work I am most familiar. I participated in several of the training workshops as well.

What I want to do is send out an invitation to dialogue. Now, as we move forward, there is an attack on the research done to examine how we view the move away from oppression to a more just society. In recent years, political attacks have been made on the attempts of minorities to get their issues addressed in academic and political venues. State political figures are seeking to ban critical race theory to eliminate cultural studies at universities and turn back the clock to a narrower view of education, such as returning to the glorification of Western civilization.

Personally, we are now fighting a real war. I see this as a positive move since much of the fight has been underground rather than aboveground. Many of the issues have simply been ignored by the dominant group. We see that those in power view democracy as acceptable because they are in the majority. In the future, this will no longer be the case. The true nature of the dominant group is now being tested. State legislatures are trying to limit the voters, who are registered, and even trying to ban critical race theory from university curricula.

Now appears to be the time to address many of the issues that were difficult to talk about because they were not given a forum. Today, the opposition has brought them to the forefront. So, for one of the few times in modern history, we have the chance to discuss in a public forum these hidden issues. I believe many of the problems that face us come from a common source. Our society was based on the premise of abuse, so it was difficult to deal with any abuse without tackling the elephant in the room—the impact of slavery. It is without a doubt that much of the abuse could have been handled, but no one had the moral right to address anything if they had accepted slavery.

Today, many of the movements, such as Black Lives Matter, responses to the public execution of George Floyd, Me Too, 21st Century Youth Leadership Movement, Leave No Child Behind, Rainbow Push, Black Alliance for Just Immigration, The Movement for Black Lives, NAACP Legal Defense and Education Fund, Coalition of Alabamians Rebuilding Education, and many others, have opened the opportunity to deal with the abuse in our culture. We are now discussing the taboo issues that only the oppressed discussed in years past. Now is the time for action.

Another strategy must be found. Oppressors continue to have the upper hand, and everything that we may do to effect change comes up short when viewed from the perspective of the monumental abuse that has been endured. Another important lesson learned is that trauma is a defining life event that combines behavior and symptoms into coping mechanisms that were initially a source of strength but now are no longer effective. The most powerful lesson is that the goal of treatment must be recovery and empowerment. Anything that is within the system that is unsafe, injurious, harmful, and not culturally relevant must be eliminated. This involves finding what has been called the *beloved community*.

Generally, the beloved community is one in which everyone is cared for. There is an absence of poverty, hunger, and hate. Although popularized by Dr. Martin Luther King Jr., the notion is generally attributed to Josiah Royce, a professor for three decades at Harvard. W. E. B. DuBois was one of Royce's students. The beloved community is one that became a focal point of the 1960s Civil Rights Movement and has been central to the work of many change agents over the years. Beginning with the nonviolence workshops and trainings of Rev. James Lawson, the Six Principles of Nonviolence presented by Martin Luther King Jr., are carried on today by Bernard LaFayette Jr. and his students in both scholarship and activism. Then there are newer organizations, such as the Selma Center for Nonviolence, Truth & Reconciliation which grew out of these workshops and training.

Now is the time for action. Therefore, another important lesson learned is that time has been the enemy. We are thousands of years behind in our thinking on how to address trauma, abuse, and injustice. Everything is time-limited. Time is a problem both in understanding the magnitude of the problem and how to attack it at its root. Another important lesson learned is that trying to play hardball with the offenders is counterproductive. But if we are honest, have we ever really played hardball with the criminal justice system? It appears at first glance that we have simply allowed the system to be unjust rather than just.

How are we to approach change? When we go back and examine how we have dealt with the problem, we learn that we have not dealt with the issues but have rather focused on notorious incidents, then forgotten them until later. There was Rodney King, now there is George Floyd. We have not done our homework, nor have we continued to work on the problem until we have a solution. We put a lot of energy into the problem, then we simply give out of steam. These issues are difficult and take time to ferret out, but we never give them the time. Our adversaries have the upper hand, and everything that we may do to effect change will come up short when viewed from the perspective of the monumental abuse that has been endured.

In addition to the lessons, there were many surprises but also a few conformations. The first conformation is that the criminal justice system does not function haphazardly but was created to function as it does. Even though we are surprised by it, we should not be. Although police misconduct may be viewed as a serious national problem by minority communities and its victims, it appears to be perpetuated by the departments and municipalities where it exists. Aggressiveness in police departments may also appear problematic in terms of media coverage, but many political entities see it as necessary to decrease street and overt crime that bothers the community. Aggressive departments are viewed as effective and efficient.

In his 2017 book, *Federal Intervention in American Police Departments*, Stephen Rushin argues that his book is the first comprehensive account of federal intervention into police misconduct. Surprisingly, a review of the literature confirms this to be the case. Why surprising? Well, back in 1994, Congress passed a little-known law called 42 USC Statue 14141 that permitted the US Attorney General to reform *troubled police departments*.

Back in the 1990s, it was determined that police officers routinely violated the Fourth Amendment to the Constitution by stopping people without reasonable suspicion, arresting them without probable cause, and using unreasonable force against them. Since that time, many of the nation's largest police departments, including Los Angeles; Chicago; Seattle; Washington, DC; Pittsburg; and New Orleans, have been included in federal oversight.

So why over this time have we continued to be driven by media coverage of notorious incidents and misbehaving individuals rather than the systematic review of police departments? Here is where the surprise comes into play. Reform efforts have been blocked by political entities and by powerful police unions. Depending on the political affiliation of the federal administrations, the intervention was either not a focus or a major one. Even during the Obama administration when federal intervention was at its height, police departments were treated with respect and departments received little in the way of punishment. Whereas police aggression has been criticized in the media, it has also been rewarded by ignoring it at every level. For example, there is no reliable data on how many people are shot by police every year.

We keep data on how many people are killed by sharks, but not by police. We have no generally accepted way to measure the prevalence of police misconduct. If the streets are deemed safe, even if departments must violate civil rights, police appear to be rewarded. Minority communities learn that people are routinely framed, documents are falsified, and officers commit perjury to send the innocent to jail. If the community is viewed as without overt crime on the streets, then the police are rewarded. Any nefarious behavior is simply forgotten until the next time. Unfortunately, for the police, the next time has included cell phone videos of the police killing George Floyd before our eyes.

Rushin stresses that policing has been the last institution to join federal intervention. According to Rushin, privately initiated structural challenges to law such as in Brown v. Board of Education, have fallen out of favor with the courts. Federal intervention is one of the few ways to challenge an unfair system. It appears that federal intervention in police departments has tried to stay under the radar. Even very problematic police departments have been treated with a great deal of respect by the federal government. Los Angeles appears to have been the department to receive the most guidance and the results are mixed.

After reviewing the sparse literature, I found that police are given enormous discretionary powers on how to apply the law with very few chances that their actions will receive any kind of review. The old and primitive brain is given unlimited access to modern-day communities. Giving anyone such discretionary power is bound to lead to actions being driven, or at least not being stopped, by internalized beliefs that have been learned since childhood.

Every prejudicial thought is allowed to come into play under these conditions. If you believe that the people you are dealing with are the scum of the earth, then what is to stop you from treating them like that and essentially eliminating them from your community. You are the *hero* in this scenario. If you believe that your infamous colleagues are doing illegal acts in these communities but this person has your back and protects you from harm, then what are you going to do about his bad behavior? I would suggest *nothing*.

Chapter 5

Building Character

When I think about character, I recall the philosophy of Coach Wooden of the famed University of California male basketball teams. Over the years, the team won eleven championships (1964, 1965, 1967–1973, 1975, and 1995). Wooden was the coach responsible for the 1960s–1970s dynasty. He was able to have the players transcend the emotions that cripple us and achieve greatness. In my opinion, he was able to show players how to defeat the *old brain* and triumph over it while using the advantages that keying into that strength provides for us. My brother Robert introduced me to the philosophy of Coach John Wooden in the early 1990s. Wooden was his hero. As he was preparing to take over a leadership role in his organization, he used the coach's philosophy as a guidepost for his organization.

Wooden emphasized strength of character as being of paramount importance. He argued that character takes years to build, but reputation can be built in a short period of time. Character is who you are internally, whereas reputation is how society sees you externally. Based on a lifetime of observations and reflections, Wooden indicated that character precedes and is more important than reputation. Character is the distinctive qualities of the person, and reputation is the general opinion of the person by others.

What seemed most important here is that character is ingrained in the individual. The thing about the sports arena is that coaches instill elements into you through repetition and rote learning. They do to and for you what the parental figure did early in your life. Sports training instills into you those characteristics needed for survival and success. Sports training can make actions second nature. You do the actions without even thinking. Wooden was one of the best at instilling these traits into you that ultimately lead to success. Wooden fashioned these principles into what he called the Pyramid of Success. I realized that it closely resembled the forty-two precepts of Ma'at—the ancient Egyptian laws, philosophy, or concepts which promote order, balance, truth, reciprocity, harmony, righteousness, morality, and justice. There are many versions of the precepts. The one that I have chosen comes from the *There's a River Flowing Through My Mind Songbook*.

Principles of Ma'at
I will not

1. Do wrong
2. Steal
3. Act with violence
4. Kill
5. Be unjust
6. Cause pain
7. Waste food
8. Lie
9. Desecrate a holy place
10. Speak evil
11. Abuse my sexuality
12. Cause the shedding of tears
13. Sow seeds of regret
14. Be an aggressor
15. Act guilefully
16. Lay waste the plowed land
17. Bear false witness

18. See my mouth in motion (against any person)
19. Be wrathful and angry except for a just cause
20. Copulate with a man's wife
21. Copulate with a woman's husband
22. Pollute myself
23. Cause terror
24. Pollute the earth
25. Speak in anger
26. Turn from words of right and truth
27. Utter curses
28. Initiate a quarrel
29. Be excitable or contentious
30. Be prejudice
31. Be an eavesdropper
32. Speak overmuch
33. Commit treason against my ancestors
34. Waste water
35. Not do evil
36. Be arrogant
37. Blaspheme (the one most high)
38. Commit fraud
39. Defraud temple offerings
40. Plunder the dead
41. Mistreat children, and
42. Mistreat animals.

This is a long list of precepts and, personally, I have or had violated many. Over the years, the leaders had tried to teach the students in our 21st Century Youth Leadership Movement Camp to obey the precepts. Should I say that as leaders we were not as successful as we hoped to be? We would spend hours teaching these concepts, and the next hour, campers would be violating them in a fit of anger.

I remember a session where we taught negotiation skills, but an argument broke out while discussing the skills, and campers were fighting as if they had learned nothing. I now realized that they had not learned anything. These principles must be ingrained. These precepts take years to master. They must be second nature. You cannot pull them up in the heat of battle; they must be wired into the old brain.

In his teachings, Wooden never dealt with the game of basketball per se, but rather with the game of life and how to succeed in that game. What I took out of this were two things: make it simple and repetitious. What Wooden showed was by making it simple, a sports training model; you could teach the principles and make them relevant. So, by simplifying what may not have been learned early in life and repeating it, you can make a difference. Instead of trying to remember forty-two precepts, the focus was on seven general precepts of truth, justice, harmony, balance, order, reciprocity, and propriety. As they sought order in the universe, the ancients sought to become one with the cosmic order.

They sought (1) control of thoughts, (2) control of actions, (3) devotion to purpose, (4) faith in the ability of their teacher to teach them the truth, (5) faith in themselves to assimilate the truth, (6) faith in yourself to wield the truth, (7) freedom from resentment under the experience of persecution, (8) freedom from resentment under the experience of wrong, (9) cultivation of the ability to distinguish between right and wrong, and (10) cultivation of the ability to distinguish between the real and unreal. In trying to teach, you must trust the teacher and the ability of the student to gain that knowledge.

Right away I knew that I did not have the trust of anyone. In a group session, I indicated that a family member would listen to anyone but the family. When confronted with this statement, the member indicated that she did not have a family and that we were all strangers to her. When I reflected on her statement, I had to give validity to it. Although we had a blood relationship, we did not know each other. We were strangers. Why should family be trusted any more than strangers on the streets?

The first obstacle that I faced was accepting the basic notion of what it means to be family. People decide on who they want to be family. I spoke with the therapist about this, and we decided that as part of the therapy, we would let people form the family that fitted their needs.

I had to accept the notion of a family which was different from the one I had accepted as a child. I decided to be more flexible and made myself useful in which ever family format I found myself.

I took the three school-aged children in the house to school every day. I cooked breakfast and made lunches for each child. I tried to make myself useful where I could. This worked well for about a year. It was during the car ride to school that I talked about character development and the precepts of Ma'at. I was trying to change the street culture to one in balance with the cosmic order. This was no small feat, but I remembered a theory from my years in graduate school, *cognitive dissonance*. In the 1960s, the theory of cognitive dissonance came into vogue as the theory that explained the unexplainable. It was the *hottest* theory in social psychology and tried to make sense of why people tended not to change detrimental behaviors in the face of evidence that they should.

In the 1960s, the study of cults had become fashionable, but understanding cultlike behavior was illusive. People tended not to change their behavior in a rational way. There was a cult that believed that the world was coming to an end on a prescribed day. They believed that only they, the true believers, would be saved by aliens on this day. In anticipation of the day, many cult members sold their belongings and planned to leave. The day came and went without salvation from the aliens, but the cult members continued to be true believers. Why in the face of contradictory evidence did they continue to believe? Leon Festinger, the proponent of cognitive dissonance, suggested that the cult members were in a state of dissonance. To bring balance back into their lives, the members had to bring the dissonance back into balance. Here you have people who have shown themselves to be foolish and to believe something foolish, but who wants to perceive themselves to be foolish? Well, how can you bring all of this into balance? For one, you can believe that your beliefs helped save the universe. You were a true believer and this has saved the world. If you accept that you are foolish, then you must make more serious changes. Believing that your beliefs were useful is the easiest manner to think, so that is the way most cult members went. Now a few accepted that they were duped and changed their beliefs about the cult and left, but this requires more soul-searching and changing.

People tend to try and look for consistency in their cognitive behavior. Take for example that you smoke and you believe that it causes cancer. If you want to live, then your behavior is dissonant. You need to bring it into balance. How will you do it? Since you believe that smoking causes cancer, then you will probably try to change your behavior. If you continue to smoke, then you will change your opinion about cancer. You will say that "I must die of something," or you question whether you personally will get cancer or whether cancer will result from smoking.

I brought up dissonant issues that challenged the students' behavior. For example, do you want to graduate from high school? If you get into legal trouble, will you graduate from high school? I got them to think about the inconsistent thoughts that they had. We talked about these issues on the way to school every morning. Was I successful? Well, that depends on how you view success and when you measure success. Two out of the three graduated from high school when it was likely that none would. The smartest in terms of grade point average dropped out in the eleventh grade. One got caught stealing and was placed in a detention center for four months and a leg monitor for two months. The other continued to ride to school and talk about the principles of Ma'at until graduation. After detention, the other student was readmitted to school and graduated.

Chapter 6

Behavioral Change

In the nefarious zone, the street criminal view appears to be the preferred perspective. It is promoted as the way to navigate the zone. Being trustworthy within the group is acceptable, but your criminal family comes before everything. Trying to change behavior to the more acceptable Ma'at perspective can be problematic. Because you are establishing character traits and changing them all at the same time, a lot is going on and, frankly, things can get confusing. I wish that I could be with you to hold your hand and tell you that you are doing well and it will all work out in the end. I really believe this because it has worked out for me. I want to be there for you and support your efforts. Believe me that flying by the seat of your pants can be scary and exhilarating all at the same time.

I know you are probably saying "Yes, but you have training in this field." Yes, I have training but more information came from me as a human being than from me as a college professor in social psychology. No matter your training, you are human and you must make a human connection first and foremost.

Begin by finding out what you, or the person in need, want. What are your goals? What do you really want to achieve? If they or you are all criminals, then you need to try and discover something more positive. Luckily, most people want something good and true to Ma'at. If they do not, do not give up. You may find that as you *talk*, you may find some hidden desires.

Talking is key to transformation. I was amazed to find that we do not talk to one another. We are constantly saying things but not necessarily to one another. So, begin your talk session by asking questions about goals and desires. I suggest that you use a small notebook or your phone for recording talking points. Have the significant people working on behavior change keep these talking points as well. Start out by writing down your goals or what you desire. For example, I want to graduate from high school. I want to be a rap artist. I want to work for Honda Inc. Write down all your goals.

Consider all your goals, then act as if you are entering a foreign country with a different language, customs, and behaviors. You may know some aspects of it, but probably only enough to get into trouble. Remember that in this nefarious culture, your designated family or gang comes before God, biological family, marriage, community, friendship, and the law. You are going to have to change your priorities if you are going to be successful in changing your behavior.

The first concept to remember is *mindfulness* which is a cognitive behavioral therapy technique borrowed from Buddhism and is flexible as a therapy. Dialectical behavioral therapy combines elements of cognitive behavioral therapy and mindfulness. Dialectical refers to the combination of two opposing notions. First is the acceptance of the reality of a person's life and behaviors, and the second is the change of solutions and dysfunctional behaviors.

Dialectical behavioral therapy is based on stages. Understanding these stages can guide you along the journey and can keep you from getting lost. The first stage is defined as crisis intervention and keeping people safe from suicide, self-harm, and addiction issues. In this stage, the therapist wants to stabilize individuals and help them gain control of their behavior. Usually, this involves an assessment of the person's mental health. If the person is stabilized, then you can proceed with treatment. In stage 2, individuals can work on their emotional pain and traumatic experiences. Here, the therapist can help identify thoughts, behaviors, and beliefs that are not helpful to a functional existence. stage 3 consists of solving issues associated with everyday life. The focus is on maintaining progress and setting achievable goals. The aim is to have the individual accept responsibility for their actions and find contentment in life. The final stage is stage 4 which involves advancing and achieving spiritual fulfillment.

My strategy is to speak with the therapist and try to make sure that the individual or self is at least at stage 3. Any previous stage is too problematic to begin. Let the professionals help if you are not at stage 3. If you do not have a therapist, then assume that you are at stage 3. You will soon discover if you are in stages 1 or 2. The person will not be able to focus. What should you do? Try to get help from a professional. If there is no help, I would start with quite simple goals. I would try not to move into stressful issues. Anything can be stressful, so beware. I would just continue to talk with the person and try to discover more about them until I feel it is safe to bring up goals.

Dialectical behavioral therapy can help the individual develop four major skills: (1) distress tolerance involves being able to feel intense emotions such as anger, grief, and shame without acting impulsively or using dysfunctional coping techniques such as self-harm, drug abuse, and violence; (2) emotion regulation involves not letting negative emotions take over and allow positive emotions to increase; (3) mindfulness allows an increased awareness of the present moment and our ability to live in the moment and allow for the positive outcomes for body awareness, regulation of emotions, and perception of self; and (4) interpersonal effectiveness allows for learning how to regulate emotions so that individuals can deal with conflict and communicate more effectively by learning skills such as listening and assertiveness.

Now, let us get back to the goals. In the last fifteen years, there has been a push to make goals more useful and measurable. As you develop goals, the key is to make them SMART:

*S*pecific
*M*easurable
*A*chievable
*R*ealistic
*T*ime-limited

For example, if an individual indicates that a goal is to be the Valedictorian of the class, but after the tenth grade, they have a C average. Is this a realistic goal? You know that this is not an achievable goal, so you get the individual to evaluate the goal. Two years are already calculated, so only two more years are in play. They may be able to graduate in the top half of the class or better if they make all *As and Bs* in the next two years. Part of the process is to get them to think about the goals, and review if they are SMART.

You can see that you do not have to have a problem to benefit from this type of thinking. Cognitive behavioral therapy techniques offer a variety of ways to evaluate your problems. Here are a few that I have personally used and found to work. First, behavioral experiments test whether your thoughts are valid or not. In other words, you test your thinking patterns to see if they produce accurate results. This strategy provides you with feedback about a particular behavior. One student felt that studying really made her perform poorly on her exams. She postulated that when she did not study, she was less worried and did better. We had her test this theory. To her surprise, she found that she did much better on her examinations when she studied.

Second, thought records, like behavioral experiments, test whether a thought is true or not. Thought records involve examining the objective evidence side by side for or against a thought. For instance, you take a driver's test and you fail. You think the tester finds you to be worthless and you will not take it again. You ask the student to look at it objectively. Many people with driver's licenses probably failed the first time. They practiced and went back. Making mistakes is normal. People are impressed when we learn from our mistakes and do better the next time. Third, pleasant activity scheduling is effective as a therapy technique. It is helpful when you are combatting depression. Try writing down in your notebook one pleasant activity that you enjoy that you would not normally do.

There are other techniques, but some have more risks because you bring up negative thoughts. I have used these three strategies with little or no problems. Speaking of risks, here are a few to consider. This therapy involves a significant time commitment. Do you have the time to commit, and do you have the time with the person? People have different mindsets, and the logical and academic mode of this therapy may not suit all. You may have to look at more spiritually-based questions. For example, you might ask, why do you think only one leper out of ten returned to thank Jesus for curing him? Because there are few follow-up studies, it is difficult to know if these therapies work and how long they last.

Overall, based on my interventions, I evaluated the behavioral change as positive. A word of caution here: I did not try to make this into a study. This was a casual moment-to-moment conversation about the students' future goals while driving them to school. First, for the five months, the ride to school included three students in the tenth grade at a local high school and the drive took around fifteen minutes. The students rode the bus home from school.

Two of the students formed SMART goals. One student was good at art and wanted to attend an art school in Florida. His goals included finishing high school at the allotted time and enrolling in art school. The other student did not speak of her goals. This turned out to be significant because I was not worried about her. She was involved in several extracurricular activities and had an *A* average in her coursework. The other student wanted to finish high school at the appropriate time and get a job for about $20 an hour at one of the local plants. She was doing well in her course work and had a *C+* average.

At the end of the tenth grade, these goals were in place for the coming academic year. One student still did not have an acknowledged goal, but again I was not worried because she continued to have a high grade point average and a positive school experience. The other student continued to pursue his goal to go to art school. The other student had improved her schoolwork and had a *B* average. As we completed the tenth grade, I was pleased with our progress and looked hopefully toward the future.

The beginning of the eleventh grade was uneventful. The three students continued their positive progress toward reaching their goals, with some goals still not acknowledged. I was incredibly pleased with myself. This was not going to be as problematic as I first imagined. The students were happy as we drove to school, with each munching on their breakfast sandwiches. Life was good.

In November, the first semester of the eleventh grade was winding down and all was going well until it was not. An adult associated with one of the students received a call from the authorities that her granddaughter was detained in the juvenile detention center. Later, I was informed that she had been stealing cell phones. The student was suspended from school and placed in the detention center until her trial. During this time, the other student dropped out of school without a known cause. The other student, who had an interest in art, continued toward his goal.

Just as all was going well, then it was not. This is important. Do not be lulled into a false sense of security. Nothing can be taken for granted until it is achieved. Not supporting and giving strokes to the ones who was doing well was a big mistake. We often focus on the ones with problems and forget the ones who seem to be doing well. Everyone could have a problem lurking around the corner. Keep this in mind.

Chapter 7

Navigating the Juvenile Criminal Zone

Determining what works in the nefarious zone is a daunting task. Of course, my focus is the juvenile criminal world and the justice system, and your zone may be some other system. From my initial foray into the zone, I was shown that I had much to learn. Understanding that my interventions were not necessarily adequate was the first lesson learned. What I observed as a seemingly problem-free existence was not necessarily indicative of one. The absence of observed negative behavior did not mean that there were no internal problems. The student with what appeared to be the best chance at success turned out to be the one with the least successful outcome at the time.

I spent little time with this student because she appeared to be doing so well. The lesson here is to not take anything for granted. Outcomes are fragile and can turn on a dime. The saying is that the squeaky wheel gets the oil, but sometimes a quiet problem needs more oil. The child that gives us no problems often gets little attention until there is a big problem before us. This child needs just as much or more attention, yet they often get extraordinarily little compared to the overtly problematic child. Also, remember that one mistake is the not end. We can come back from mistakes. There have been people who have graduated after many years. Just keep your eyes on the prize.

Once you are in the nefarious zone, there are many issues that need to be addressed if you are to leave this zone successfully. The second lesson learned is that you must fight on at least two fronts, the criminal world and the system created to adjudicate it. You are not the first in this zone, and the interrelatedness of the problems suggests that there are interventions already in place. Your strategy for success is to learn as much about this world and identify what help and assistance are available for you.

Now, I have several suggestions to get you started, but if you can come up with strategies on your own, please use them. Learn as much as you can about the street culture and code that your child may have internalized and accepted. Try to combat this culture by articulating what your beliefs and values are and why you believe them to be more valuable than the street ones. Learn what the zone has in terms of preventive, maintenance, and probation programs. Try to find out what the success rates are and how they are being implemented. Try to discover if the programs are being monitored and how. I have examples of some programs that appear to be working. See if these types of programs are being used in your zone. Also, do you have information about the connection between the regular school system and the juvenile criminal system?

I reviewed the literature through googlescholar.com. I looked up the history of the criminal justice system and the relationship between the code of the streets and juveniles. The relationship between education and the juvenile system was also examined. I was also interested in how girls fared in the system because most of the juveniles that I had contact with were female. I wanted to learn as much about this world as I could. Now I am trained in research so this was easy for me. You may have more problems with this approach so try reading more books than journal articles in the beginning. Most research has a target audience and recent research does not include much jargon. The research is accessible to a wider and general audience.

I found out that a significant portion of those in the juvenile criminal system is known to have education-related disabilities and are eligible for special education and related services. Under the Federal Individuals with

Disabilities Education Act (IDEA), learning disabilities, undiscovered disabilities, or emotional disturbances are included. The most common are specific learning disabilities and emotional disturbances. Other disabilities could include blindness, deaf/hearing impairment, speech and language impairment, traumatic brain injury, autism, orthopedic impairment, and multiple disabilities.

According to Burrell and Warboys in their article on special education and the juvenile justice system, specific learning disabilities are defined as disorders in one or more of the basic psychological processes involved in understanding or in using language, spoken or written. These disorders may show themselves in an imperfect ability to listen, think, speak, read, write, spell, or do mathematical calculations. It is important that you understand how juveniles are being identified, evaluated, and referred in your area. School districts and other public agencies are required to seek out youth with the mandated *child find obligation*. We know that with limited funding and personnel that this mandate is often not met. You must ask difficult questions. What is being done in your area to identify those youth with disabilities and disturbances and get them help? Juveniles need an advocate. That advocate may be you.

So let us consider that you have accepted the role of advocate. What do you do? The first thing I did was try to learn as much about the juvenile criminal justice system as I could. I looked up books and articles on googlescholar.com. I am affiliated with a university so I could use my university identification, but you can create a user identification or go to your public library. I used the public library a great deal because I am old-school and just love paper books more than e-books.

Once I had learned about the history of the juvenile system, I made an appointment to see a probation officer. I had notes in my book, but you can have them on your phone or wherever. You may have information about your program, but ask more pointed and detailed questions, such as what the names of the intervention programs used are.

Identify the programs by their name, such as the Reaffirming Young Sisters' Excellence (RYSE) program. RYSE was a program identified by Zahn and her colleagues in an evaluation of which programs work for girls. Which group is targeted? Adjudicated twelve to seventeen African American girls are recruited for the program. Is this program based on race, gender, and/or for the hard-core juveniles, the middle-range offenders, those just initiated, or as a preventive for those with problems that lead to delinquency?

What is known about the reliability and validity of the programs? RYSE's results are from a randomized controlled study. It was deemed to be both reliable (measures the same girls the same way over time) and valid (measures what it is purported to measure). Some have pre-posttest with controls and pre-posttest without controls. You do not need to know the statistics behind each of these methods, but you need to know what data gives them confidence that the program works.

What does the program do? This program attempts to prevent girls from returning to the juvenile system or entering the adult system. The recruitment process is of paramount importance here. Were the appropriate criteria used to obtain the girls? Who could benefit from the program? The intervention includes home visits by probation officers, individual case plans, concrete funds for emergencies, life skills courses, programmatic teen pregnancy services, and therapy. Does the program work? While the girls are present in the program, it appears to work, but after the program, much less so. The lesson learned is that follow-up programs are needed. Is the program residential with more intensive work or an outpatient day program? This is crucial when each program is evaluated. The system has an idea of what works, but the funds to implement the programs are usually not there. The limitations of the program need to be identified and outlined.

You need to know all the nuts and bolts of the program. Once you have the information needed, you will have some idea if this program is going to be successful. Here you may not have any options. You may have to participate in the program even if you feel that it will not work. You participate, or you must receive a less positive option. This is how the system works. If you must participate, then you need to work up your own program using what you have learned. You will try to implement your program along with the juvenile program. I suggest that you employ Sun Tzu.

The world of Sun Tzu comprises a multitude of shifting, interrelated parts. The nefarious zone can be said to include grounds. I like to think of these grounds as an example of the types of areas that you might have to navigate. This is more symbolic than real. It was useful to view these zones as where you engage your enemy which could be parts of the criminal justice system and/or the criminal zones where the individual might get ensnared.

I found that when you used the terms associated with warfare, you got the attention of the potential offender. Instead of talking about going to the crime-infested neighborhood, you call it *death ground*. You might associate each area with a ground. There is the apartment or dormitory, there are the places where kids hang out, like the mall, there is school, friends' houses, and so on. You know whether the person likes to take risks and loves danger. We call these types of people *thrill junkies*. But when I referred to the places they liked to go as death grounds, they were forced to view their behavior in a different way.

I tried to label each of these travels and living spaces as one of the nine grounds. First, there was the apartment. I referred to it as *connected ground*. I wanted the offender to have interactions with college students rather than the usual dropouts. Because the apartment was near a university, it seemed the perfect place. Because of the security and key entry access with codes, it seemed secure and safe. Later, it was discovered that the building had an unsecured back door which allowed entry to everyone. When I reported it, nothing was done until much later to secure it.

What was perfect in the beginning turned out to be less than ideal. Everyone had access to the building. Residents simply stayed after being evicted and no one bothered to check. When you entered the building, you smelled the aroma of drugs in the hallways. Although there was a police presence in the building, he seemed fixated on certain apartments. A friend provided a safer space. The lease was not renewed because things were viewed differently after living in the space.

Chapter 8

Human Trafficking and the Nefarious Zone

Over twenty years ago, I first heard the term *nefarious* at a conference on trafficking. The young female moderator talked about a zone in the desert outside of the United States' borders that was a dumping ground for mainly dead women. Most of these women were missing vital organs, such as kidneys, livers, and ovaries. She spoke about horrors in plain sight. We were dutifully horrified, but most of us thought of it as pretty much an exaggeration to make a point to her audience. She wanted us to know that this was serious and that we should think about the possibilities if these actions continued unabated.

In 2014 when I was in California, the issue of trafficking surfaced again. Because I knew a family that had a member that might have been trafficked, this time I had a personal connection. Trying to understand more about the phenomena got me started on this journey, I have tried to cloak these travels in mystery to protect the innocent. As I stated earlier, I try to combine cases and change genders and ages to mask the identities of the offenders.

When one of our offenders was reunited with her biological family, a corresponding separation was made with the criminal family. The most surprising issue for me was that separation from the criminal family was more traumatic than separation from the biological family. The offender had traveled with the criminal gang for only a few months.

How did they connect with her in such a powerful way in such a short period of time? It took only two weeks on the streets to affiliate and have allegiance to the gang. The gang kept in touch with her for more than a year. They never actively tried to recruit her but they stayed in touch. They were within a cell phone's reach of her during this time. She never went back to them, but you can see that the gang made it extremely easy for her to move back if anything went wrong with the new arrangements.

What do I mean by the gang? A gang is a group of people who live and travel together for the purpose of committing criminal acts. They usually engage in theft, drugs, and prostitution. Based on what the offender told us, they use the underage members as shields. The younger ones take the fall for the criminal acts and shield the older members. California officials suggested that this was common and that if you lived in states other than California, Florida, or Texas where trafficking was known to be a problem, you were behind the *eight ball*. You were ignorant and, frankly, thousands of years behind the traffickers.

In ways unknown to us, these criminal gangs are associated with human trafficking. At-risk girls on the streets are the most vulnerable. I am a fan of Asian dramas so I knew about fictional human trafficking but saw it as a historical view of what happened thousands of years ago. I had no idea that it still existed. According to California officials, the world of human trafficking exists today and is a multibillion-dollar enterprise. Human trafficking is the trade of humans for the purpose of forced labor, sexual slavery, or commercial sexual exploitation. You can find out about it on the internet and several books are available on the subject. Surprisingly, trafficking includes forced marriage, extraction of organs and tissues, and surrogacy. I was reminded of the lecture many years ago that I had not believed.

This is the trade in people, especially women and children, and it does not necessarily mean the movement of people from one place to another. This knowledge is outside the understanding of most of us in the Western world. You might start out with the perspective that women are valued less in the Eastern world. If you are honest, the reality is that girls and females, in general, are less valued in all cultures. If you are poor and a minority, you may well be abused in any culture. Trafficking is complicated and convoluted in that the victims are evil, and the perpetrators are viewed as innocent. A male visiting a massage parlor is acceptable, but the girls who work in the parlor are viewed negatively. I found out that there are excursions to Asian countries for the sole purpose of having access to trafficked girls. Several of my otherwise law-abiding male associates found this fact acceptable. Some had even traveled to these countries. They saw the girls and women as making money and being agents of strength in their countries. My discussions with them made some reconsider their beliefs, but, frankly, most had extraordinarily little sympathy for the victims. This very fact makes the idea of ending this system of exploitation very unlikely.

I decided to try and learn more about trafficking even though just dealing with the juvenile criminal justice system was a daunting task for me. What I discovered keeps me up at night. What is the solution? Is there a solution? Maybe someone who reads this book will discover the answers. I found out from the authorities that approximately 1 percent of the trafficked ever get rescued. Therefore, the knowledge we have is inadequate at best and erroneous at worst. Yet we believe that we understand how they operate, how they gain the advantage, and the impact that this life has on the victims. To the extent that this knowledge represents one percent of the victims and 99 percent is unknown presents serious problems, but you work with what you have.

Getting out of the life of a trafficked person can be a long process. The exploitation that occurs is at a high level and reflects the long-term existence of this crime. The traps involve interacting with the vulnerable and capitalizing on their weaknesses. Make no mistake, these are high-level predators with long personal criminal histories and networks with long organizational histories. We are literally outnumbered and without much to combat them at a realistic level. When you think about it, you often feel overwhelmed by the sheer magnitude of the problem. Can there be any hope for these modern-day slaves?

Here is what I learned from observations and interviews. First, they do not appear to rely as much on violence as previously thought. They rely more on gaining trust and providing favors for the victims.

I learned that they routinely provide cell phones if you need one. They flatter victims and give them money, no strings attached. They set up traps at malls, theaters, hair and wig stores, cell phone stores, and any place where young people hang out. The internet is one place with many traps, but the internet is probably the least likely place to meet these predators. They do not want to leave any footprints, so face-to-face connections are likely the preferred contact mode. They pose as a boyfriend, provide false job opportunities, and act as a parental figure. They consider this as grooming. It would be much better if they were the evil and violently abusive individuals portrayed in the media. It seems that in real life they come in the guise of helpers rather than harmers. Their kindness to the victims is what enslaves them, not the violence.

In plain sight, you can find the exploited ones at hotels, residences, massage parlors, farms, construction sites, domestic venues, hospitality sites, even in schools. Yes, many continue in school as they are trafficked after school hours. The innocent observers simply look the other way. They are getting workers for cheap, and they never ask hard questions. The ones who are supposed to care simply turn away from the offenses. One victim remarked that no one ever looked her in the eyes. So, health care workers and other workers in these industries are unaware of what is happening. If you look in the eyes, you will know that something is wrong. No one ever looks.

Poverty plays an important role in how this plays out. In terms of impoverished societies, girls have more economic value in sexual trade than as wives and mothers. According to the rescued, it is the family that has sold them into slavery. They really have no one that they can trust. Housing is a big issue as well. Where do they go to escape? Often the traffickers are trusted more than the family. The websites on human trafficking stated that in 2014, the International Labour Organization estimated that forced labor alone profited these gangs by $150 billion. In 2012, an estimated twenty-one million persons were modern-day slaves. Even if not officially viewed as slaves, over half of the 215 million young workers are in hazardous sectors, forced sex work, and forced street begging.

Since approximately 1 percent are rescued, this is what we have been able to learn from them about the effects of trafficking. In ways that are just being discovered, this sort of victimization is stored throughout the brain. This enslavement involves all the senses as well as the emotions. Although we are each unique and experience trauma differently, there are some basic facts that set this form of suffering apart from other forms of trauma. Trauma appears to change the brain. It gets *rewired* and can even impact the developing brain of children. For example, the hippocampus is part of the brain that recalls the memory and differentiates between past and present experiences. It has been shown that abuse distorts how the hippocampus operates, and past and present experiences become confused. The victims think something that happened in the past is happening in the present. This type of confusion makes it difficult for the person to carry on a normal existence.

We have discussed the problems of the old brain with its fight-and-flight responses. Trafficking seems to make it even more difficult for the old brain to operate in a normal manner. As a result of the extreme effects of trafficking, those initiated into the life become hardened by the nefarious environment and learn to survive as predators themselves. It is estimated that many who start out as victims eventually become abusers themselves. Exposure occurs along a continuum. Understanding the wounds is beyond most treatment facilities. In their work on identifying and treating the wounds of trafficking, Clawson, Salomon, and Grace have tried to understand the trauma and its aftermath. Much of what is presented here is based on their work.

Ronald Fairbairn wrote a series of articles on the attachment of abused children to their abusers in the 1940s and presented them in his 1952 text, *Psychoanalytic Studies of the Personality*. He viewed the lack of love and unmet needs as leading to the emotional attachment to the person abusing them. The defense of dissociation leads the child to protect themselves from fully realizing what has happened to them. The controversy here stems from whether children and adults can be viewed in the same manner when dealing with abuse. It is one thing to be a victim of child abuse and another to be a victim as an adult. The aftermath of abuse has been found to carry serious side effects. One that has been baffling is Stockholm syndrome because it has been viewed in adults as opposed to children.

Stockholm syndrome has been observed as a reaction experienced by some abuse victims that extends beyond the actual kidnapping or hostage-taking incident. This information comes in part from Wikipedia. The syndrome is defined as a condition where captives develop a psychological bond with their captors during the hostage period. During their time together, emotional bonds are formed between captors and captives. This appears to be irrational in view of the danger the victims face at the hands of the captors.

First observed and used by the media in 1973 when four hostages were taken during a bank robbery in Stockholm, Sweden, the victims defended their captors. The police were viewed as having little care for the hostages' safety, so the feelings of the hostages were reasonable. However, the syndrome is paradoxical because having sympathetic feelings toward captors is the opposite of the fear and anger which an onlooker might feel toward them.

This is a *contested illness* because of the doubt about the legitimacy of the syndrome. Nevertheless, four key components characterize the syndrome: (1) the victims, especially of sexual abuse, develop positive feelings toward the abuser; (2) no previous relationship exists between victim and abuser; (3) a refusal to cooperate with the police and other government authorities unless abusers are police officials; and (4) the belief in the humanity of the abuser when they appear to hold the same values as the victim. Here you just are not sure what is going on. Are victims chosen because of their susceptibility?

The Stockholm syndrome has never been included in the Diagnostic and Statistical Manual of Mental Disorders or DSM, the standard tool for the diagnostic of psychiatric illnesses or disorders, due to the lack of a consistent body of academic research in the area. According to the FBI, around 5 percent of hostage victims show evidence of this syndrome. However, of the 1 percent of rescued trafficked persons, a large percentage appears to have the syndrome. Numbers are problematic here, but something goes on with the emotional bonds between victims and abusers that need to be studied.

Most adult victims are likely to experience post-traumatic stress disorder rather than Stockholm syndrome. It appears, however, that there could be elements of both when you are trafficked. Post-traumatic stress disorder (PTSD) and other psychological and physical include (1) cognitive confusion, blurred memory, delusion, and recurring flashbacks; (2) lack of feeling, fear, helplessness, hopelessness, aggression, depression, guilt, and dependence on the captor; (3) social anxiety, irritability, cautiousness, and estrangement; and (4) increased physical effects, development of health conditions because of food and sleep restrictions and exposure to the elements, plus added physical issues, including tattooing, piercings, and cuttings.

Post-traumatic stress disorder (PTSD) was originally created to understand what had happened to war combatants and disaster victims. It was discovered that after experiencing trauma during war and disasters, victims had similar post-traumatic problems, such as flashbacks, nightmares, trouble sleeping, and intrusive thoughts. These problems were such that normal everyday functioning was disrupted. Therapists discovered that victims started to self-medicate with drugs and alcohol. The victims used many methods to escape these problems. Most had little success in dealing with the problems and little success in holding a job, paying bills, and reintegrating into society.

The impact of trauma exposure is not well understood, but exposure is believed to exist along a continuum of complexity from a single less complex incident to repeated and intrusive incidents involving stigma or shame. It is unclear how the brain handles the far end of the spectrum or how much time and effort is needed to recover.

What is known is that time is the enemy of treatment. It seems to take much more time to recover than it takes to develop the effects of the trauma. There appear to be many barriers and challenges to both identifying victims and getting them help. It takes much more time to undo the damage than to create the problem. Given that the therapy modalities are intensive and require time, very few victims ever get the long-term treatment needed. It is known what works, but the time and money involved make these therapies less accessible to the many who need them. Providing culturally relevant materials to highly disturbed individuals is awfully expensive. Grounding therapies, the management of dissociative systems, and desensitizing therapies may be delivered as individual and group treatments but require highly trained therapists who are not available in many states.

There are logistical and psychological limitations to the availability and accessibility of mental health services. The very nature of the abuse involves shame, confidentiality, lack of insurance, citizen documentation, and requirements to report that cause problems. Establishing trust given everything that has happened is problematic. Mandated treatments can be counterproductive. Often, these treatments, which the offenders call *Mickey Mouse*, are not adequate for the task. Secrecy is the trademark, so a complex set of strategies has been put into place to mask events. It is almost like an onion that is being peeled one layer at a time.

Successful treatment modalities rely on *frank* disclosure and working through problems. Much of this is not possible given the nature of the offense. There are two types of services provided that appear to have had some success: (1) trauma-informed services that are appropriate for all systems of care, and (2) trauma specific services that treat the actual symptoms of physical and sexual abuse.

Trauma-informed services are committed to providing services in a welcoming and appropriate manner. These types of services are often provided in homeless shelters, substance abuse treatment centers, criminal and juvenile justice systems, mental health programs, medical centers, and community health centers. Although the services are provided in many venues, nothing can be taken for granted. Services must be investigated. The specialized services of trauma-specific centers are rarely available without cost and can be extremely expensive. Some of them cost up to $25,000 a year. They are usually residential and provide a unique environment for the client. They have an extremely qualified staff and are probably successful, but there are little data available on their success rates.

Afterword

An Invitation to Dialogue

Breaking down the code of silence within and outside of the police departments is a formidable task. What this journey has taught me is that trying to create a new format is not necessary. We already have the methods in our arsenal. The immensely powerful tools we have used for over fifty years to create change are still available to us. When immersed in an issue, we are often helpless and feel powerless, but our work in civil rights, peace and justice, participatory research, CARE, women's studies, health, and change should give us hope. If we think back to the work of Paulo Freire and the oppressed in Brazil, the Highlander Center and Rosa Parks, participatory research in Tanzania, the 21st Century Leadership Movement, the Selma Voting Rights Movement, and the community health advisor model out of the University of Alabama at Birmingham, we understand that we have the tools to address this formidable issue.

Forming coalitions that include groups from dominant areas in the community must be the goal. Participatory research is a self-conscious method of empowering people to take effective action toward improving conditions in their lives. It is not new for people to raise questions about their condition or to actively search for a better way of doing things. What we are looking at is how these actions can be viewed and carried out as intellectual activities that deserve our attention. These organizational efforts have as their goal rational liberatory events.

Cast in the mold of research, the knowledge of what is needed for a better life and what must be done to attain that life is made clearer. Knowledge becomes a crucial element in enabling people to have a say in how they would like to see the world put together and run. Putting research capabilities in the hands of the deprived and disenfranchised allows them to buy into the changes so they can transform their lives themselves.

This is an invitation to dialogue. We want to change police actions and culture. Yet as we begin this journey, we discover that we have little data on which to make critical decisions. The United States keeps extraordinarily little data on local police behavior. The first area is to gain data. How do we get more data? What is necessary to learn more about police behavior? We have the media that focuses primarily on the notorious actions of the police, but what about the day-to-day information?

Next, how do you get a buy-in to make a cultural change? So far, the government has opted to negotiate amicable settlements out of court with police departments. Have these quiet closed-door negotiations worked? I would suggest that they do not appear to work. So, what is needed instead? What is needed to get a buy-in from the affected communities? Which other constituencies must be included in the buy-in?

In their article, "Taking Diversity and Inclusion to the Next Level," VISIONS, Inc. asks the question, "Is reconciliation possible?" For the entire article, go to www.visions-inc.org. Reconciliation is a process of transformation that examines both sides of a conflict. This transformation is critical to formulating any effective strategy of change. VISIONS, Inc. argues that reconciliation is an interactive process occurring at four different levels: the personal (values, beliefs, feelings, attitudes, opinions, and bias), the interpersonal (treatment, relationships, behaviors, communications, and microaggressions), the institutional (policies, practices, rules, procedures, and systems), and the cultural (worldview, stories, climate, media, public opinion, norms, unwritten rules, and group dynamics).

To dialogue, we must have a common language in which to communicate. This agreed language must be broad enough to handle all the issues put forth. Since I know more about VISIONS, Inc, it is the organization that I have chosen to focus on in this afterword. It is not the only organization doing this work, and what I want to stress again is that I am not making any judgments here. I simply am familiar with this organization's work.

VISIONS, Inc. stresses that modern racism is often not malicious in its intent but rather is defined as "the expression in terms of abstract ideological symbols and symbolic behaviors of the feeling that blacks are violating cherished values and making illegitimate demands for changes in the racial status quo." For example, when I participated in a VISIONS, Inc. workshop, several participants discussed that they did not view minorities in a negative manner. They saw them as just humans, but further discussions revealed that when they drove through minority neighborhoods as children, their parents made sure the windows were up and the doors were locked. They never said anything to the children, but these actions were observed and locked away in the subconscious. This suggested to the children that we are now in a danger zone and must act accordingly.

I remember participating in a workshop session with the CEO of a major corporation who discussed how minorities, which included about 10 percent of the staff, segregated themselves while eating in the cafeteria at lunch. We asked him if he noticed that 90 percent of the nonminority staff were segregated at lunch. He did not notice that the majority were eating together. That was normal in his organization. He only noticed the 10 percent that was eating together.

When we pointed out that the dominant group did not want to interact with the minority group, he remarked that this was not true. He had never been taught to hate minorities, but now as he thought about it, he realized that he had not been allowed to interact with them, either. He had grown up in a poor community near minorities. But he was discouraged from the meeting, talking, and socializing with them.

For the first time, he realized how the minorities in his organization banded together for support in his company. He now understood that they ate together for a reason. His task became how to make them feel welcome in his company and not to try to make them interact with others when they did not feel welcome. The majority of members are not aware that many times the burden of making interactions work is placed on the shoulders of the least powerful people in the organization. The work should be on the shoulders of the powerful, like the CEO.

As I completed my observations, I decided to expand the dialogue to two individuals who were representative of the type of work being done today. I decided to interview these people to learn what was on the minds of people on the battlefield. The first woman is a friend of over thirty years who is a PhD agent of change from a social change theory and transactional analysis approach. She grew up in the segregated South and has vivid memories of losing friends to violence. Her young life was filled with turmoil around the fight for freedom, but she was supported by a religious family that believed in the power of God to make changes. In 1963, after four little girls (Cynthia Wesley, Denise McNair, Carole Robertson, and Addie Mae Collins) were murdered in Sunday school by a bomb detonated only a block from her Sunday school, she channeled that raw hurt and rage into a passion to fight injustice. She has her own organization and is also a senior consultant with VISIONS, Inc.

Her take on the work with police departments is that very few want to deal with the hard issues. In her thirty years of work, she can recall only about five departments requesting help from her organizations. Most of these departments had been mandated to seek help so the work started out with an adversarial relationship and little chance to be successful. She strongly trusted the work with the four levels of oppression, analysis, and change that included the personal, the interpersonal, the institutional, and the cultural. She did not really believe that it mattered where you began, but that each level had to be addressed.

For example, many organizations start at the institutional level and change practices, rules, and policies, but find things remain the same. This is because police are given a great deal of latitude to address the problems, so personal and interpersonal issues come into play. She believes that addressing the factors that determine what is in the best interest of the departments is likely to provide for areas of change. What is going to improve the way in which you can most effectively carry out your job? She feels strongly that police departments could benefit from the training offered by VISIONS, Inc., but does not view it as likely that departments will avail themselves of the training.

When asked why, she indicated that because the culture of the police departments is militaristic and aggressive, sensitivity training is viewed as problematic. Teaching the police to be sensitive and value the feelings and attitudes of the communities they interact with is viewed as undermining the effectiveness and efficiency of the departments. She would focus on trying to get departments to see that this work is in the best interest of the departments and will in the end create a better work environment for everyone. They expect you to beat up on them, they do not expect you to want to see things from their perspective. I am saying we are in this together. We must make this work, and if you are not on board, how can it work?

The next person to be interviewed is a retired university constitutional law professor who is now working with a team of lawyers fighting for the civil rights of defendants. Over the years, she has helped countries write their constitutions and been an advisor to countries dealing with new constitutions. Since retiring, she now has the time to devote to these issues. Although she has not dealt with departments in terms of making changes, she has been involved with suing them when they violate the constitutional rights of citizens. For example, one police department was sued for stopping drivers who had tinted windows. Although the tinted windows may not be illegal and there was no presumption that the windows were related to crimes, the stopping affected minorities more than any other group.

Her take on the problem is that dealing with the police is a massive undertaking. The police are held responsible for more issues than they can realistically be expected to deal with effectively. When you dial 911, you are calling for help. If you are not calling for a medical emergency, what you get is the police. You need help, but there is no other help. The police must deal with domestic issues, mental health issues, and other noncriminal matters. This is outside of the purview of their mission, and they are not trained to handle this myriad of problems, and the tasks are massive.

We have been getting by on the cheap, and the mountain of unmet needs keeps growing. The police need more and more revenue so they target the neighborhoods that will give them the most revenue with the least amount of grief. Think about the problems they will receive if they target the wealthiest communities in the area. The wealthiest women are targeted coming from church and randomly stopped for traffic violations. Can you imagine the outcry in the community? So minority communities get targeted. The poorest and the most vulnerable must come up with the revenue.

Bibliography

Batts, Valerie A. "Is Reconciliation Possible: Lessons from Combating 'Modern Racism.'" www.VISIONS-Inc.org, 2016.

Borderline Personality Disorder, https: www.mind-diagnostic.org/free.

Braga, Anthony A, David M Hureau and Andrew V Papachristos. "An Ex Post Facto Evaluation Framework for Place-Based Police Interventions." *Evaluation Review* 35 (6), 592–626, 2011.

Briggs-Myers Personality Test. https://www.16personalities.com/free-personality-test.

Burke, Ronald, Judith A Waters and William Ussery. "Police Stress: History, Contributing Factors, Symptoms, and Interventions." *Policing: An International Journal of Police Strategies & Management,* 2007.

Burrell, Sue and Loren Warboys. "Working Together: Building Local Monitoring Capacity for Juvenile Detention Centers." *Report,* 1997.

Burrell, Sue and Loren Warboys. "Special Education and the Juvenile Justice System." *Juvenile Bulletin.* Juvenile Justice Clearinghouse, 2000.

Coalition of Alabamians Reforming Education. Changed later to Rebuilding (CARE). http://care.freeservers.com

Clendenning, John. *The Life and Thought of Josiah Royce*. Vanderbilt University Press, 1999.

Coach John Wooden's Official Website. https://coachwooden.com.

Denma Translation Group. *Sun Tzu, The Art of War*. Boston and London: Shambhala, 2002.

Diagnostic and Statistical Manual of Mental Disorders. https://www.psychiatry.org

Dialectical Behavior Therapy. www.verywellmind.com. www.goodtheraphy.org

Durr, Virginia Foster. *Outside the Magic Circle: The Autobiography of Virginia Foster Durr*. Fire Ant Books, Paperback edition, 2013.

Fairbairn, Ronald. *Psychoanalytic Studies of Personality, 1952*. Routledge, 1st ed., 1994.

Festinger, Leon. *A Theory of Cognitive Dissonance*. Stanford University Press, 1959. www.goodtheraphy.org>leon-festinger.

Freirc, Paulo. *Pedagogy of the Oppressed: 50th Anniversary Edition*. Bloomsbury Academic, 4th Edition, 2018.

Highlander Center. https://highlandercenter.org.

King, Martin Luther Jr. *Strength to Love*. New York: Harper and Row, 1964.

LaFayette, Bernard Jr. and Kathryn Lee Johnson. *In Peace and Freedom: My Journey in Selma.* Lexington: The University Press of Kentucky, 2013.

Law Enforcement Misconduct Statute 42 U.S.C. _14141 Department of Justice 34 U.S.C. 12601. justice.gov. (a .gov website belongs to an official government organization and the lock or https:// means you've safely connected to a .gov website.

Nefarious Zone. www.thefreedictionary.com

Participatory Research. https://www.participatorymethods.org.

Principles of Ma'at-Kemet Experience. https://www.kemetexperience.com

Rushin, Stephen. *Federal Intervention in American Police Departments.* Cambridge University Press, 2017.

Sanders, Hank. *Death of a Fat Man: A Novel.* Selma: Imani Way Enterprises, 2004.

Selma Center for Nonviolence, Truth & Reconciliation @ the Healing Waters Retreat Center. www.selmacenterfornonviolence.org.

SMART Objectives. https://www.clearreview.com

Southeast Institute for Group and Family Therapy. https://www.seinstitute.com

Toure, Faya Rose & Friends. *There's A River Flowing Through My Mind Songbook: A Unique Historical Journey Through Black History Using a Collection of Music and Stories.* Selma: Imani Way Press, 2014,

Walker, Deborah J. "On Whose Shoulders I Stand." *Kids in Birmingham 1963*. September 2013. http://perspectives.

Young, Andrew. *An Easy Burden: The Civil Rights Movement and the Transformation of America, 2nd ed.* New York: Harper-Collins, 2008.

Zahn, Margaret A, Jacob C Day, Sharon F Mihalic, Lisa Tichavsky. "Determining What Works for

Girls in the Juvenile Justice System: A Summary of Evaluation." *Crime & Delinquency* (55, No. 2), 266–293, April 2009.

Zinn, Howard. *A People's History of the United States.* New York: Harper-Collins, 2010.

CPSIA information can be obtained
at www.ICGtesting.com
Printed in the USA
BVHW081104080323
659961BV00006B/309